© Aladdin Books Ltd

Designed and produced by
Aladdin Books Ltd
70 Old Compton Street
LONDON W1

First published in the
United States in 1988 by
Gloucester Press
387 Park Avenue South
New York NY 10016

ISBN 0 531 17095 0

Library of Congress Catalog
Card Number: 87-83078

Certain illustrations originally published in
The Closer Look Series

Contents

Arctic Lands

Kate Petty

Illustrated by
Maurice Wilson

small world

Gloucester Press
New York · London · Toronto · Sydney

The Arctic year

The lands of the Arctic form a rough circle between the ice of the North Pole and the first trees of the northern forests. These Arctic lands are known as the tundra.

Early spring
March-April
Heavy snowfalls

Late spring
May-July Snow starts
to melt. Days long

Summer
August-September
Plenty of wildlife

The tundra covers one tenth of the world's land surface. The long winters and short summers of the Arctic make this "cold desert" unlike anywhere else. For a few months each year it is full of wildlife.

Autumn
October-November
Lakes freeze

Early winter
November-December
Snow and ice

Late winter
January-February
Cold and dark

Saxifrage makes new plants by sending out long shoots.

Plant life on the tundra

Each year the snow and ice of the tundra are melted by the warm sunshine. Only the top layer of the earth is warmed. Underneath, the earth is hard and frozen. A few sorts of plants can survive there. They grow close to the ground, out of the wind. Some have hairy leaves and stems for warmth. Perennials (plants that come up year after year) do better than annuals (plants that live for only one year).

Reindeer moss grows very slowly. It is the main food of caribou.

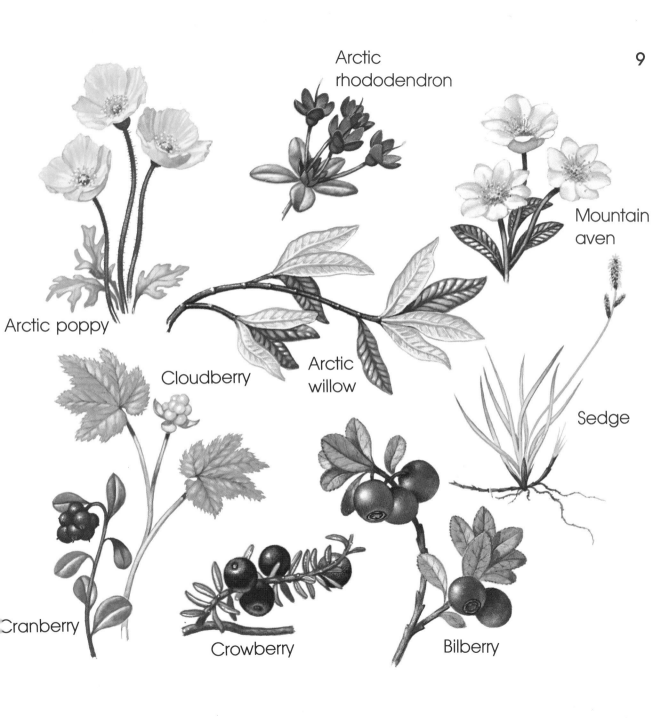

Arctic poppy

Arctic rhododendron

Mountain aven

Cloudberry

Arctic willow

Sedge

Cranberry

Crowberry

Bilberry

Permanent residents

Not many creatures can survive the harsh conditions of the tundra all the year around. The Arctic winter is too cold for them and there is not enough food.

The creatures on these pages are the permanent residents of the Arctic. They have thick furry coats to keep out the cold. Some of them turn white for the winter. They are hard to see in the snow.

Winter and summer coats

Stoat

Arctic hare

Ptarmigan

Arctic fox

Permanent residents
of the tundra

Gyrfalcon

Snowy owl

Arctic fox

Raven

Stoat

These animals and
birds eat only
plants

Redpoll

Meadow vole

Ptarmigan

Lemming

Arctic hare

Musk-ox

Spring arrivals

Long summer days and remote nesting places
make the Arctic a good place for birds to
breed. Hundreds of different birds start to arrive
from the beginning of April.

Barnacle goose

Bear goose

Black-throated diver

Lesser scaup

Red-breasted goose

Great northern diver

Knot

Sandhill crane

King eider duck

Many of these birds are waterfowl. Some of them have flown all the way from Africa and the Orient. The Arctic tern comes from the South Atlantic, 11,000 miles away.

Blue snow goose

Snow goose

Rock pipit

Bewick swan

Oldsquaw duck

Northern phalarope

ay phalarope

Caribou are good swimmers. On land their large hooves are suited to wet or snowy ground.

Regular visitors

During the winter, caribou live in the forests below the tundra. As soon as their calves are born they make their way to the tundra in great herds. They graze on reindeer moss and other lichens. Caribou is the name given to these animals in North America. In Europe and Asia they are called reindeer.

Large predators

Wolves prey on the caribou. They follow the herd in well-organized packs, killing weak or injured members.They are powerful and intelligent hunters, found in most parts of the Arctic. Grizzly bears live in the forests and tundra. They don't often attack large prey, but feed mostly on berries, roots and leaves. The wolverine, lynx and red fox sometimes come to the tundra in search of food.

Grizzly
bear

Wolverine

Lynx

Red fox

A time of plenty

By midsummer the tundra is full of life. Warm
sunshine and water from the melted snow
make the flowers spring up. Millions of insects,
including bumblebees, appear with the plants.
Ponds and lakes are alive with fish and
waterfowl.

Sandhill crane

Musk-oxe

Red fox

Red-bre
mergans

Whistling swans

Ground squirrel

Eider duck

Tundra animals

Caribou

Canada geese

...dsquaw duck

The little lemming is very brave. It will fight when cornered, however large the enemy.

Lemmings

Almost every hunting animal in the Arctic eats lemmings. They are small, furry rodents, about five inches long. In summer they live underground. In winter they burrow under the snow and spend much of the time asleep.

There are two sorts of lemming, brown and collared. Collared lemmings like this one turn white in winter.

Lemmings breed very quickly. One
mother can have fifty babies in a year.
Every fourth year there is a lemming
population explosion. Bands of
lemmings go off in search of food. The
following year fewer lemmings are born
and the four-year cycle begins again.

Snowy owls need
plenty of lemmings
to feed their young.
They may not breed
at all in a poor
lemming year.

Birds depart for the South

End of the summer

The last of the summer sun ripens all the many sorts of berries that grow on the tundra. They provide the animals with vitamins before the winter. Wolves, foxes and bears eat them, as well as birds and mammals.

By the end of September all the migrating birds will have left for warmer countries. The coats of many animals start to turn white. Only the ground squirrel hibernates. It curls up in a grass-lined nest, deep in a bank.

Hibernating
ground squirrel

Winter in the Arctic

After the end of August many parts of the Arctic
hardly see the sun. Snow covers everything.
The tundra is cold and dark and quiet.

The large animals in their thick
winter coats can search for
food above the snow.

Small animals burrow below the snow where it is warmer in winter. They can still find insects and plants to eat. Stoats and weasels hunt the voles and lemmings in their burrows.

Below the snow it is usually 7°C warmer than on the surface. The temperature stays at about −3°C.

The last great wilderness

The Arctic is one of the last great wild places left in the world. There are still parts of it that have not been explored by humans.

Caribou eskimo

The changing tundra

Now the natural balance between the people, the animals and the wildlife of the Arctic is changing. Planes fly overhead. Already mines and pipelines and roads have been built to extract the oil and precious minerals that lie beneath the frozen earth. The harsh beauty of the tundra is in danger of being spoiled forever.

PRINTED IN BELGIUM BY
proost
INTERNATIONAL BOOK PRODUCTION